A STONE PROMISE

A STONE PROMISE

BY CARA REICHEL

LANDMARK EDITIONS, INC.

P.O. Box 4469 • 1402 Kansas Avenue • Kansas City, Missouri 64127
(816) 241-4919

For Anne Hamilton
who believes in gnomes and me.
My first book is Pearl's second.

COPYRIGHT © 1991 BY CARA REICHEL

International Standard Book Number: 0-933849-35-4 (LIB. BDG.)

Library of Congress Cataloging-in-Publication Data
Reichel, Cara, 1974-
    A stone promise / written and illustrated by Cara Reichel.
    p.   cm.
    Summary: A young stonecutter vows to create a magnificent statue for an impoverished village whose downtrodden inhabitants can no longer see beauty in anything around them.
    ISBN 0-933849-35-4 (lib. bdg.)
    [1. Sculptors — Fiction.   2. Statues — Fiction.]
    I. Title.
    PZ7.R2635St   1991
    [Fic] — dc20
                                    91-15059
                                    CIP
                                    AC

Editorial Coordinator: Nancy R. Thatch
Creative Coordinator: David Melton

Printed in the United States of America

Landmark Editions, Inc.
P.O. Box 4469
1402 Kansas Avenue
Kansas City, Missouri 64127
(816) 241-4919

329336

A STONE PROMISE

Cara Reichel is a poet and a musician. When one reads her text and sees her striking illustrations, it becomes evident that her work as a writer and illustrator is influenced by her poetic nature and her love for music.

The tonality of Cara's narrative and the fluid rhythms created within the structure of her sentences play as sweet music to the reader. Cara doesn't merely tell a story; she skillfully weaves a ribbon of places and events into a vibrant mosaic of moods and scenes. While one may enjoy reading the prose of A STONE PROMISE in solitude, the lines cry out to be read aloud so the music of the language Cara has composed can be shared and enjoyed to the fullest.

The graceful lines of Cara's illustrations offer the sensation of poetry and music in a visual form. Her black and white silhouettes are perfect for the nature of her story. They help create a shadow play of light and darkness that we as readers feel privileged to experience and enjoy.

— David Melton
Creative Coordinator
Landmark Editions, Inc.

WINNER

1990
WRITTEN &
ILLUSTRATED
BY... **AWARD**

The small fishing village of Collure lay at the foot of the steep cliffs that thrust themselves up between the high moors of western France and the sea. The road from across the moors twisted crookedly down the face of the bluffs and through the village to the beach, where its muddy ruts finally faded in the pebble-strewn sand. There at water's edge, fishnets were spread out to dry in the evenings and fishing boats stood lined up, ready to leave at the call of dawn.

The owners of the patched nets and leaky boats passed their nights under patched quilts and leaky roofs, thinking of little else than their tired backs and half-filled stomachs. To them, sunrise was no more than a dreaded call to work and sunset nothing but a reminder that they were one day closer to the ends of their lives.

In the bleakness of their days and the emptiness of their nights, the people of Collure no longer saw beauty in anything around them. They never stopped to notice the delicate glow of fishing lanterns reflected in the early morning fog. They never looked upward to enjoy the majestic view of the towering cliffs. And they were blind to the everchanging colors that moved restlessly on the currents of the ocean.

There was simply no space left in the hearts of the villagers to appreciate beauty, no time for anything except scraping out a meager living. It had been like that for hundreds of years. It would remain the same for generations to come — or so it seemed.

Strangely enough, hope for the people to ever see beauty was to come from one of the least likely of persons: a street urchin of no more than ten years of age, clothed in a thin ragged shirt and pair of tattered pants. In the chill of an autumn morning, this ragamuffin boy made his way through Collure, following narrow streets that smelled of fish gut and hard times. He had begun his days in this way for as long as he could remember.

The boy soon entered the market square and began to weave between the piles of crates and mildewed canvas. He was extremely hungry. As he passed near a basket of freshly caught fish, he reached out, grabbed a small mackerel by the tail, and slipped it under his shirt. He thought his theft had gone unnoticed, as it usually did, but not this morning.

"Hey, you! Put that fish back!" shouted an angry merchant.

The boy instantly bolted through the crowd and ran up the street. Hearing the voice of the pursuing merchant, the child darted around a corner and up the

main road out of the village. He didn't stop until he reached a plateau on the rocky cliffs — farther from the village than he had ever been before.

There the boy leaned against a stone wall and gasped for air. When he finally caught his breath, he glanced back to see if he were still being followed. He was relieved to find the fish merchant was nowhere in sight.

The child had no idea where he was; he had never seen the wall. But prompted by his need to hide, he scrambled up the trunk of a nearby tree and crawled onto a limb to peer over the top of the enclosure.

Before him was a place unlike any the boy had ever seen: an old monastery, inhabited only by the monks who prayed in seclusion behind its cloistered walls. In the courtyard were several stone buildings, but the boy's attention was drawn to the chapel at the end of a walk. Its solid blocks of stone stood in curious contrast to the fragile translucence of its stained glass windows.

The sound of the merchant's angry voice interrupted the boy's thoughts. He jumped down into the courtyard and ran to the chapel. With his grubby hands, he opened the door wide enough to slip inside.

As he looked about for a hiding place, he was awestruck by what he saw. The patterns of colored light that streamed like jewels through the windows and across the wooden benches dazzled his senses. Then he saw them: in the spaces between the windows, twelve life-sized statues stood as sentinels along the walls. He had never seen anything like them, and he felt compelled to move nearer to the stone figures.

Suddenly the chapel door was flung open. The strong hand of a constable grabbed hold of the boy's shoulder and spun him around.

"That's the thieving urchin!" yelled the fish merchant.

When the boy tried to pull free, the mackerel dropped from beneath his shirt and fell to the floor.

"And there's the evidence!" the merchant exclaimed. "Arrest that boy!"

"Come with me!" the constable ordered, and he started pulling the boy toward the door.

"What is the trouble, Constable?" a monk asked as he entered the chapel.

"Nothing to concern you, Father. We've just caught a thief who was hiding in your chapel."

The monk stepped forward and looked down at the boy.

"Is this small lad your thief?" he asked in disbelief.

"Yes! He's the one who stole my fish," the merchant said. "Good thing we caught him before he had time to steal anything from you. Now he'll be put in prison where he belongs."

The monk bent down and picked up the mackerel.

"It's not a very big fish," he said. "Are you hungry, lad?" he asked, noticing the child's thin body.

The boy didn't answer.

"It is my understanding, Constable, that your prison is already overcrowded," the monk said. "Surely, no one would miss the addition of such a small child. If you'll leave the boy here, I will make sure he never again steals from the merchant."

"Once a thief, always a thief!" the merchant snarled. "If you keep that boy, he'll steal you blind."

"I am willing to take that chance," the monk replied calmly as he handed the fish to the grumbling merchant.

"Then he's yours, Father," the constable said, letting go of the boy's arm.

After the men were gone, the monk said to the boy, "I am Father Bernard. What is your name, lad?"

"They call me Remi," the boy replied sullenly.

"Where are your parents, Remi?"

"I was told my mother died when I was born. My father drowned at sea. But I don't need any family. I can take care of myself."

"I think you will like it here," the monk told him.

"A prison is a prison," the boy replied, looking up at the stone walls.

"But this is not a prison," Father Bernard said. "There are no locks on our doors. You may leave anytime you want. If you choose to stay here, we will give you food, clean clothes, and a warm place to sleep. But, in return, you must promise never to steal."

Remi looked up and gazed directly into the eyes of the monk. The boy had never seen such a friendly face or been offered such kindness. Then he looked back at the statues. The stone figures still intrigued him. Remi knew he could not leave them — not yet.

"All right," the boy finally agreed, "I promise not to steal."

As Father Bernard led Remi toward the dining hall, he thought the boy's decision to stay was based on hunger. That was true — the child did need food.

But Remi had other hungers, too, ones that even he did not understand. He knew only that he had to see the statues again. Above all else, he had to touch them with his hands.

In the weeks that followed, Remi awakened each morning before sunrise, as the monks did, to attend morning prayers and begin a full day's work. He helped with the chores, taking his turn at carrying water from the well, tending the gardens, and scrubbing the floors.

During each day, time was also set aside for lessons. Although Remi had not expected those, he became an apt student, interested in everything the monks taught him. Most of all he liked lessons with Father Bernard, and a mutual fondness soon grew between the boy and his mentor.

Father Bernard was pleased with the thoroughness of Remi's work. But one thing puzzled the monk. For periods of time each day, Remi would be missing. One morning Father Bernard found the boy's bucket and scrub brush in the hallway by the chapel. When the monk opened the door and stepped inside, he saw Remi was there, rubbing his hands along the curved lines of one of the statues.

"What are you doing?" the monk asked.

"I am just looking at the statue," the startled boy replied quickly.

"But, why are you touching it?"

"Because I can see it better with my hands," Remi explained. "I am feeling the cuts made by the stonecutter. If you touch it, Father, you'll see what I mean."

Father Bernard reached out his hand and felt the figure.

"I feel only the surface of the stone," he said.

Then Remi looked at Father Bernard and said a very strange thing: "It's not alive."

"No, it's only a statue," the monk replied, not knowing what else to say.

"Yes, that's all it is," the boy agreed.

The conversation ended, and Remi returned to scrubbing the floors. But in the mind of Father Bernard, the boy's words were not easily forgotten. He wondered what Remi had meant when he said, "It's not alive."

Several days later two monks came to Father Bernard.

"One of the knives is missing from the kitchen," Brother Michel told him.

"And a chisel and hammer have been taken from the carpentry shop," added Brother Paul.

"Who would take these things?" Father Bernard wondered aloud.

"Last week I saw the boy Remi take a log of wood from the shed and carry it to his room," Brother Michel said.

"I will look into the matter," Father Bernard assured them.

That evening Father Bernard knocked at the door of Remi's room. As he waited the monk could hear Remi quickly moving things about. Finally the boy opened the door.

"Remi," the monk said matter-of-factly. "I have been told a knife has been taken from the kitchen and tools are missing from the carpentry shop. Someone has also taken wood from the shed."

"I didn't steal them," Remi explained quickly. "I just borrowed them."

"But, why would you do so?" the monk asked.

The boy bent down and raised the covers from the side of his bed. Reaching under the slats, he pulled out a carved wooden statue and timidly handed it to Father Bernard.

The statue was the figure of a man, with arms upstretched and reaching as if he were trying to gather all of the world's beauty in his hands. The expression on the wooden face was one of utmost joy. It was a rough carving, to be sure, but the figure seemed so alive that as Father Bernard held it in his hands, he could almost feel a heartbeat pulse through the body of wood.

"Did you carve this, Remi?"

"Yes, Father," the boy replied.

Then Remi pulled the knife and tools from under his bed and held them out to the monk.

"No, you keep them," Father Bernard said. "They are yours. You have earned them. From this day forward, you will not have to sneak wood from the shed. You may go there anytime and choose the finest logs for your carvings."

And so it was.

The following years were good ones; years in which Remi learned the meaning of beauty. And as he came to understand that meaning more and more, the beauty he felt planted itself deeper within him and continued to grow.

Remi expressed his sense of beauty through his creations. He carved many statues which the monks joyfully placed throughout the monastery.

As often as their duties would allow, the monks stopped by the carpentry shop to watch the marvelous wooden forms take shape. Under Remi's skillful hands, a mother and child, an old man shivering in the cold, a saint, or one of the apostles would emerge. All the monks were amazed at the lifelike quality of the pieces.

"I sometimes think I can see your statues breathe," Father Bernard remarked to Remi one day.

"That is because I have cut into the life of the wood," Remi replied.

"But the stone statues in the chapel don't have the same feeling of life," the monk said.

"I know," Remi agreed. "They were cut without considering the life that is within the stone itself. That is why they are only statues. They are not alive."

One afternoon Remi asked Father Bernard for permission to leave the monastery for a few hours.

"There is a huge stone at the top of the cliffs," the boy explained. "I want to climb up and see it."

"It is dangerous on the high cliffs," Father Bernard warned. "The wind from the ocean can be fierce. You could be blown from the rocks."

"I will be careful," Remi promised. "But I must see the stone!"

"Then I will go with you," Father Bernard said.

Remi was surprised, for like the other monks, Father Bernard rarely stepped outside the walls of the monastery.

As the two of them climbed the side of the rocky cliffs, Remi learned that Father Bernard had been right about the wind. The sudden, unpredictable blasts made the ascent hazardous. But foothold by foothold, the boy and the monk made their way upward and finally reached the top.

"The stone is even bigger than I thought!" Remi exclaimed when he neared it. Then he pressed forward against the wind and eagerly stretched out his hands to touch the stone.

"Oh, Father, it is a great stone!" Remi cried out. "I feel powerful life within it! It will make a magnificent statue! And this is the perfect place for it to stand."

"But, why up here — in this lonely place?" the monk asked.

"Because all the villagers will be able to see it from below," Remi answered knowingly.

"Someday," the boy vowed, "I will cut into the life of this stone and create a beautiful statue for the people of Collure! Once they look upon such a statue, their eyes will be opened to the beauty that is all around them."

Father Bernard listened to the fervor of Remi's words, and he believed them to be true.

One wintry afternoon, when Remi was fifteen years old, Father Bernard brought a stranger into the carpentry shop.

"Remi, this is Pierre Renaud, one of the most famous stonecutters in all of France," said the monk. "I have been showing him the wooden statues you carved. Monsieur Renaud is considering taking you on as an apprentice."

"Will you teach me to be a stonecutter?" Remi asked eagerly.

"A little at a time," Monsieur Renaud answered. "The cutting of stone is very different from carving wood. It requires many years of training."

"Remi learns quickly," Father Bernard assured him.

"That is good," Renaud replied. "Then it is settled. Pack your belongings and be prepared to leave at dawn tomorrow morning."

Remi was surprised. "Do you mean I will have to leave the monastery?"

"Of course," Renaud answered. "We go to Paris. I have been commissioned to create a statue of Moses for the grand cathedral there."

"Do you think I should go?" Remi asked Father Bernard.

"I think you must go, Remi. It's too great an opportunity for you to miss," the monk replied.

Before leaving the next morning, Remi stopped by the chapel to tell his old friend good-bye.

"I have something for you, Father," he said, and he handed the monk a small wooden chest.

Father Bernard opened the lid. Inside the chest was the first wood carving Remi had made years before.

"When I become a master stonecutter," Remi said, "I will return to Collure. From the great stone on the high cliffs, I will cut a statue just like the carving. This, I promise."

Father Bernard accepted Remi's promise. He conferred his blessings upon the young man and told him good-bye. Remi turned quickly and hurried to the front gate, hoping Father Bernard had not noticed the tears in his eyes.

Remi's breath hung in the cold air like fog as he climbed into Monsieur Renaud's cart. Then the two of them, master and apprentice, traveled across the French countryside, sleeping in beds and eating at tables that were not their own.

When they finally reached Paris, Remi could not believe he was seeing such a glorious place. How different the city was from Collure. He had not known there could be so much color and life in the world. In the streets vendors were everywhere, selling everything from exotic fruits to bolts of brightly colored cloth. Jugglers tossed silk balls high into the air and caught them again and again. Bards roamed among the crowds, playing harps and pipes, and praising the joys of life with their songs.

Remi could hardly wait to see Monsieur Renaud's studio. When he entered the room, he was immediately fascinated by a huge stone that stood there. He wanted to reach out and touch it, but he resisted the urge.

On a worktable nearby rested a clay model of the statue which was to be cut from the stone. With great anticipation, Remi approached the model and looked closely at it. He was disappointed. The figure appeared lifeless, having none of the inner energy he thought a fine statue should possess.

The following morning work on the statue began, along with Remi's first instructions in stonecutting. Monsieur Renaud taught the young man the proper way of holding the chisel against the stone and the correct technique for controlling the powerful blows of the hammer.

Before Remi started to work, he stood before the massive piece of marble and placed his hands upon it. Then he moved all the way around it, feeling each side and corner.

"What are you doing?" Monsieur Renaud asked rather impatiently.

"I am feeling the life within the stone," Remi replied.

Renaud was puzzled by the statement. But he asked no more about it as he watched Remi raise the chisel to the surface of the stone and begin wielding precise blows with the hammer. Monsieur Renaud had never seen stone fall away with such ease.

In the days that followed, Pierre Renaud observed his apprentice with amazement and a bit of envy. There seemed to be a bond of life between Remi and the stone itself. Renaud had no doubt that Remi had been born to cut stone.

When the rough cutting was finished, Monsieur Renaud took over. During the sculpting of Moses, Remi watched every move made by the master stonecutter. He observed with such intensity that his teacher often felt uncomfortable.

When the statue was near completion, Renaud became quite irritable. He frequently paced back and forth with a scowl on his face.

"Something is not right!" he said repeatedly.

"There is life within the stone," Remi finally told him, "but you have not yet cut into it."

Monsieur Renaud was furious. He threw his tools to the floor.

"Show me what you mean!" he demanded.

Remi approached the statue. He closed his eyes, and with sensitive fingers, he touched the figure's face. Then he picked up the chisel and hammer and began making delicate cuts into the stone.

Renaud watched with astonishment as Remi's cuts brought forth the vibrant face of Moses. Then Remi's chisel changed the flow of the robe across the statue's shoulders, revealing the strength of muscles and the softness of flesh beneath. Sure that he had seen the statue breathe, Monsieur Renaud gasped.

When Remi finally completed his work and stepped back, there was no doubt which man was the master stonecutter and which one was the apprentice.

Remi and Monsieur Renaud worked together for many years. By the time Renaud retired, Remi had become even more famous than the old master. Each statue the young man cut was different, more dynamic in some way than the one before. Hard stone glowed lustrously soft in his skilled hands, revealing the alabaster skin of a Madonna or the glistening, pure face of an angel. Those who looked at the pain in the faces of his *pietàs* felt a deep sadness within themselves for the suffering revealed in the stone.

Demand for Remi's beautiful statues was enormous. He worked at all hours, day and night, to complete his commissions, but he did not mind. His life was dedicated to his art. He lived through his creations, signing each one with the only name he had — *Remi*.

In the years that followed Remi traveled the many countries of the continent. He created statues for great cathedrals and palaces. Cities proudly displayed his works, and patrons of the arts boasted of having a *Remi* in their homes. By the time Remi was forty years of age, he was considered to be the finest stonecutter in all of Europe.

Nevertheless, Remi did not forget the promise he had made long ago to Father Bernard. Every year he vowed to journey to Collure and cut the statue from the great stone on the cliffs. But as each year passed and he became more famous, he continued to postpone his return to the small fishing village.

Finally old age began to take its toll on Remi. The muscles in his arms were not as strong as they had been in his youth; his hands became twisted and gnarled with arthritis. Even so, Remi ignored the warnings of his pain-filled body and continued to cut stone. He was pushed on by his desire to create a work of ultimate beauty.

But after he had completed a colossal statue in Rome, Remi realized he no longer had the strength to challenge another piece of stone. He lay down his chisel and hammer for what he believed would be the last time.

Thinking he would be content to live out his remaining years in quiet seclusion, Remi returned to his home in Paris. There he found rest, but no peace of mind, for as the days passed, his thoughts turned more and more to the village of Collure and the promise he had not fulfilled.

When he slept images of the great stone haunted his dreams. Then, one night Remi saw the image he had dreaded most, but somehow knew would eventually come. He saw Father Bernard standing at the foot of the bed. The expression on the monk's face was one of kindness and understanding. Remi would rather it had been one of disappointment and disapproval, for he might have been able to withstand that. But the gentle face of Father Bernard filled him with a shame he could not endure. Although he no longer had the strength to cut the great stone, Remi knew he must return to Collure at once.

It was late autumn. The chill of winter was already in the air as Remi's coach traveled along the rugged road across the moors, heading toward the village he had not seen for more than fifty years. The steel-gray sky, absent of clouds, held no welcome for the tired old man.

It was dusk by the time Remi arrived at the gate of the monastery. As he climbed from the coach, a cold shiver stirred through his body. He couldn't resist pausing for a moment to look down the road. The village appeared the same as he had remembered it — nothing had changed.

A feeling of remorse flooded through Remi. Once he had possessed the talent and strength to change the lives of the villagers, but he had waited too long. He had used his talent and expended his strength to create beauty for strangers in other places, while ignoring the needs of his own people.

As usual the gate of the monastery was unlocked. Remi entered the courtyard and walked with some difficulty to the door of the chapel. As he stepped inside the sanctuary, he felt as cold and alone as he had the first time he entered the place years before. Only now the room was darker: the pale light of evening had dimmed the colors of the stained glass windows, and the stone statues stood in silent shadows.

When the side door opened, Remi was startled. For a moment he thought he saw Father Bernard enter the room. Then he realized that the monk who stood before him was not his old friend.

"I am Father Philippe," the monk said kindly. "May I help you, old man?"

"I am a friend of Father Bernard," Remi said.

"But the good Father has been dead for twenty years," the monk told him.

"I knew him a long time ago," Remi said, "when I was a boy."

"And what is your name?"

"I am called Remi," the old man replied quietly.

"*You* are Remi — the great stonecutter?" the monk exclaimed in excitement. "Please, wait here, Sir."

The monk hurried from the chapel. When he returned he held out a wooden chest to Remi.

"Father Bernard said you would come back someday. He told us we were to give this to you."

Remi took the chest in his hands. He knew what it contained — a small wooden figure — now a painful reminder of his broken promise. Although he did not want to look inside, he could not stop himself from raising the lid. When he saw the carving, tears filled his eyes, and he staggered to a bench and sat down.

"Are you all right?" inquired Father Philippe.

"I have not eaten since morning," Remi replied. But he knew the pain he felt was not due to lack of food.

As it had happened many years before, Remi was led into the dining hall to eat with the monks. After evening prayers in the chapel, the old man was ushered

to the room where he had slept as a boy. And there, memories of his childhood and his unfulfilled promise engulfed his mind.

Finally, when he could stand no more, he grabbed his cape from the rack, wrapped it around his shoulders, and hobbled out of the building. He made his way across the courtyard and opened the gate. Then he followed the wall to the cliffs and began to climb toward the top.

A storm at sea blew the wind at a fierce pitch. Rain poured in sheets, making the wet rocks beneath Remi's feet even more slippery. But he was determined to continue his dangerous climb. When he at last reached the top, Remi staggered to the great stone and fell against it in anguish and despair.

At sunrise the following morning, the people of Collure began to awaken. Wives stirred peat fires and cooked sparse meals for their families. Fishermen ate in somber silence, then trudged toward their boats. Merchants began to open shops. And women carrying baskets soon crowded into the market square, their children following close behind.

It was a little girl who first noticed the strange new sight that stood high on the cliffs. She tugged at her mother's skirt and pointed upward. When the woman looked up, she gasped in astonishment. Where the huge stone had once been, the figure of a man now stood silhouetted against the sun. His arms were up-stretched and reaching as if to gather all of the world's beauty in his hands.

One by one, the others in the market square looked up and were amazed by what they saw. News of the statue spread quickly, and soon all the villagers were staring at the incredible sight. Then, as rays of morning sunlight intensified and surrounded the statue, the people no longer saw cold stone, but a presence as warm as life itself.

Just as Remi had foretold, the powerful beauty of the statue struck a chord of recognition deep within the hearts of the villagers. It awakened in them a longing for beauty in their own lives.

Now, everywhere the people looked, beauty in an array of forms presented itself and overwhelmed their senses. They began to notice the brilliant colors of the sunrise and the reflection of light dancing on the ocean waves. They saw the delicate perfection of their children's faces — faces which were now filled with hope.

For the first time in a long time, the villagers smiled at one another. Soon their laughter could be heard from the beach to the high moors.

Hearing the sounds of joy coming from the village below, the monks hurried from the monastery. They, too, were awestruck by the sight of the wondrous statue. But they had no doubt who had cut it.

When the monks told the villagers who had created the statue, the people wanted to thank Remi for his precious gift. But the stonecutter could not be found. Fearing that the old man had fallen ill or been injured, Father Philippe and two other monks climbed the cliffs to search for Remi. When they reached the top, they saw no sign of him there.

Then, as the monks stood looking at the statue, they became puzzled. Even if Remi had been able to hold the tools in his gnarled hands, they wondered how he could have created a work of this size overnight. And how strange that no blocks or chips of cut stone were scattered on the ground. Father Philippe was even more puzzled when he ran his hands across the statue. He found no marks on the surface of the stone to indicate that chisel or hammer had ever touched it.

Most amazing of all was the statue's face. It was unmistakably that of Remi the Stonecutter, and from it radiated an expression of ultimate joy.

Remi's promise in stone had been fulfilled.

Remi was never seen again in the village of Collure. But since that time long ago, there have been many legends about the great stonecutter and his stone promise.

Some say, when Remi finished the statue, he returned to Paris to live out his days. Others say, after his work was finished, the old stonecutter fell exhausted from the cliffs and his body was washed out to sea.

But there are those who sit by evening fires and tell that Remi never fell to his death or left the village at all. They believe the stonecutter's body and spirit merged with the great stone that night and created a figure of everlasting life and beauty. They say Remi stands there on the high cliffs, forever suspended in stone, to remind the people of Collure never to forget to see the beauty that surrounds them.

THE NATIONAL WRITTEN & ILLUSTRATED

— THE 1989 NATIONAL AWARD WINNING BOOKS —

Lauren Peters
age 7

Michael Cain
age 11

Amity Gaige
age 16

Dennis Vollmer
age 6

Lisa Gross
age 12

Stacy Chbosky
age 14

Adam Moore
age 9

Michael Aushenker
age 19

Problems at the North Pole
Written & Illustrated by Lauren Peters

the Legend of SIR MIGUEL
written and illustrated by MICHAEL CAIN

WE ARE A THUNDERSTORM
written and photographed by amity gaige

—THE 1987 NATIONAL AWARD WINNING BOOKS—

JOSHUA DISOBEYS
Written and Illustrated by Dennis Vollmer

THE HALF & HALF DOG
written and illustrated by LISA GROSS

WHO OWNS THE SUN?
—written & illustrated by— STACY CHBOSKY

—THE 1989 GOLD AWARD WINNERS—

BROKEN ARROW BOY
WRITTEN AND ILLUSTRATED BY ADAM MOORE and his friends

GET THAT GOAT!
WRITTEN AND ILLUSTRATED BY MICHAEL AUSHENKER

Students' Winning Books Motivate and Inspire

Each year it is Landmark's pleasure to publish the winning books of The National Written & Illustrated By... Awards Contest For Students. These are important books because they supply such positive motivation and inspiration for other talented students to write and illustrate books too!

Students of All Ages Love the Winning Books

Students of all ages enjoy reading these fascinating books created by our young author/illustrators. When students see the beautiful books, printed in full color and handsomely bound in hardback covers, they, too, will become excited about writing and illustrating books and eager to enter them in the Contest.

Enter Your Book In the Next Contest

If you are 6 to 19 years of age, you may enter the Contest too. Perhaps your book may be one of the next winners and you will become a published author and illustrator too.

BY... AWARDS CONTEST FOR STUDENTS

— THE 1988 NATIONAL AWARD WINNING BOOKS —

WHO CAN FIX IT?
written & illustrated by
Leslie Ann MacKeen

ELMER the GRUMP
— written & illustrated by —
ELIZABETH HAIDLE

Taddy McFinley and the Great Grey Grimly
written & illustrated by
Heidi Salter

Leslie Ann MacKeen
age 9

Elizabeth Haidle
age 13

—THE 1986 NATIONAL AWARD WINNING BOOKS—

Strong and Free
written and illustrated by
Amy Hagstrom

ME AND MY VEGGIES
WRITTEN AND ILLUSTRATED BY
ISAAC WHITLATCH

WORLD WAR WON
WRITTEN & ILLUSTRATED BY
Dav Pilkey

Heidi Salter
age 19

Amy Hagstrom
age 9

— THE 1985 GOLD AWARD WINNERS —

Winners Receive Contracts, Royalties and Scholarships

The National Written & Illustrated by... Contest Is an Annual Event! There is no entry fee! The winners receive publishing contracts, royalties on the sale of their books, and all-expense-paid trips to our offices in Kansas City, Missouri, where professional editors and art directors assist them in preparing their final manuscripts and illustrations for publication.

Winning Students Receive Scholarships Too! The R.D. and Joan Dale Hubbard Foundation will award a total of $30,000 in scholarship certificates to the winners and the four runners-up in all three age categories. Each winner receives a $5,000 scholarship; those in Second Place are awarded a $2,000 scholarship; and those in Third, Fourth, and Fifth Places receive a $1,000 scholarship.

Walking is Wild Weird and Wacky
written and illustrated by
Karen Kerber

THE DRAGON OF ORD
written and illustrated by
DAVID McADOO

Isaac Whitlatch
age 11

To obtain Contest Rules, send a self-addressed, stamped, business-size envelope to: THE NATIONAL WRITTEN & ILLUSTRATED BY... AWARDS CONTEST FOR STUDENTS, Landmark Editions, Inc., P.O. Box 4469, Kansas City, MO 64127.

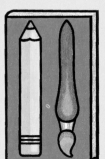

Karen Kerber
age 12

David McAdoo
age 14

Dav Pilkey
age 19

THE WRITTEN & ILLUSTRATED BY... CONTEST
— THE 1990 NATIONAL AWARD WINNING BOOKS —

Aruna Chandrasekhar
age 9

Anika Thomas
age 13

Cara Reichel
age 15

Jonathan Kahn
age 9

Jayna Miller
age 19

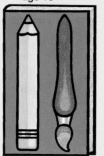

OLIVER and the OIL SPILL
written and illustrated by ARUNA CHANDRASEKHAR

Life in the ghetto
written and illustrated by ANIKA D. THOMAS

A STONE PROMISE BY CARA REICHEL

— THE 1990 GOLD AWARD WINNERS —

PATULOUS THE PRAIRIE RATTLESNAKE
written and illustrated by JONATHAN KAHN

TOO MUCH TRICK OR TREAT
WRITTEN AND ILLUSTRATED BY JAYNA MILLER

Winning the Gold Award and having my book published are two of the most exciting things that have ever happened to me! If you are a student between 6 and 19 years of age, and you like to write and draw, then create a book of your own and enter it in the Contest. Who knows? Maybe your book will be one of the next winners, and you will become a published author and illustrator too.

— Jayna Miller
Author and Illustrator
TOO MUCH TRICK OR TREAT

EMS CHILDREN 811 JOHNSON
   2010
Johnson, Dinah
Black magic

Shamblee   03/08/2010

Black Magic

Dinah Johnson

illustrated by

R. Gregory Christie

Christy Ottaviano Books

HENRY HOLT AND COMPANY ★ NEW YORK

Black is big
like a star-filled sky

and tiny like the
sparkle in my daddy's eye

when he hugs me
with his strong black arms.

Black is LOUD
like my best tap shoes
making happy noise
with every move,

and black is quiet
like a butterfly.

Black is **delicious** like
the deepest, darkest chocolate
that melts in my mouth
in a moment.

Black is quick
and black is slow
like the winding road.

Where does it go?

Black is PROUD
like my sister
at her graduation

and silly
like my Uncle Nathan
with his fuzzy mustache
that tickles me.

Black is **silky**
like my puppy, Ebony.

Black is shiny
like my brother's
new car.

Black is
scary
and
exciting
like when you go
far, far, far
inside
a tunnel.

Black notes make music
on a plain white sheet.
Black words make stories
that we can
speak out loud . . .

...or keep in our hearts
to erase the blackness
of being apart sometimes
from the people we love.

Black is surprising
like the stripes on a zebra's hide

or a sudden kiss.

And black is a wish.

Black is majestic
like a baobab tree
that you can see

if you go with me
to Mali

in my dream.

My hundred black braids
make a spiderweb
around my head,

and Mama's voice is
black and sweet
as I fall asleep.

Black is older
than a rainbow.

It is blue and blue
and **bluer** still
than any sea.

Black is the magic
the blue black magic,
the always magic
inside of me.

For Christy Ottaviano, for believing in my work
For Niani Feelings, for believing in me
For Jon Russell Washington, for believing in the magic
For Richard Vig Ross, Jr.,
Douglas L. Johnson, Jr.,
and Douglas L. Johnson, Sr. (1933–2008)
. . . just because . . .
—D. J.

For Naziah Hagan
—R. G. C.

Henry Holt and Company, LLC, *Publishers since 1866*
175 Fifth Avenue, New York, New York 10010
www.HenryHoltKids.com

Henry Holt® is a registered trademark of Henry Holt and Company, LLC.
Text copyright © 2010 by Dinah Johnson
Illustrations copyright © 2010 by R. Gregory Christie
All rights reserved.
Distributed in Canada by H. B. Fenn and Company Ltd.

Library of Congress Cataloging-in-Publication Data
Johnson, Dinah.
Black magic / Dinah Johnson ; illustrated by R. Gregory Christie. — 1st ed.
p.   cm.
ISBN 978-0-8050-7833-6
1. African Americans—Juvenile poetry. I. Christie, Gregory, ill. II. Title.
PS3560.O3747B57 2010   811'.54—dc22   2009009219

First Edition—2010 / Designed by April Ward
The artist used acrylic gouache on illustration board
to create the illustrations for this book.
Printed in September 2009 in China by SNP Leefung Printers Ltd.,
Dongguan City, Guangdong Province, on acid-free paper. ∞

1 3 5 7 9 10 8 6 4 2